E*D*I:

Getting Paid

INVOICING AND THE 810 DOCUMENT

By

Christopher E. Cancilla

Contents

NEW and REVIEW

There are EDI Analysts, EDI Programmers, EDI Developers, EDI Business Developers, and Analysts, and, well, the list goes on. What are you? What do you want to be?

Personally, I bill myself as an EDI Geek. Never an expert. Why not an expert? Because if you tell a prospective customer or employer you're an expert at something, and you are needed to do that specific thing and have no idea how to accomplish it, are you really an expert? No, in my opinion there can never be an EDI Expert. There is always something to learn or something you have never done before.

Being an expert throws up a flag that you have seen it all and done it all and....AND...fixed it all and made it all work in harmony with the universe.

How is it possible for you to be an expert under that definition? You can't be! So, what are you? An EDI Geek. Defined as someone who enjoys EDI, is well versed in it use and, in its capabilities, and can circumvent their way around obstacles.

That's me. Someone who is told the system cannot do that, and I make it happen. EDI is not being a programmer, it is creative programming at its finest. Coaxing the data to behave in a specific way is what an EDI Developer does.

In Book #1, an EDI Introduction, we talked mainly about the envelope of the X12 document. The ISA, the GS, the ST and their counterparts at the bottom of the page. We walked through what each and every element meant and why it was needed. We even mentioned that the ISA is the ONLY segment in the world of EDI that is exactly 106 characters in length, why that is a universal constant. Lastly, in Book One, we discussed the 997 or the Functional Acknowledgement. How to read it and why it is important.

So, we will not be talking about those documents, segments, elements or related data. Let's talk about something really important, specific EDI documents.

EDI Invoices versus Mailed/Fax'd Invoices

Sending an invoice to a customer is common and a great idea if ultimately getting paid for selling something is your goal, they purchase a product and you send an invoice, they pay it and cycle complete! Right?

Well, if you mail an invoice and they mail a check time is wasted. Yes, NET 10 means something to a payor, but it also means something to the payee.

Is it pay within 10 days of the invoice date or is it pay within 10 days of the date you received the invoice in the mail. Fine line and some people - companies - like to walk that tight rope every month, with every invoice.

Rather than paying when it is received, it is scheduled to be paid on the date it is due and sending a check takes up to a week and in theory, a standard pay time of NET 30 could mean 6 or 7 weeks until you see the money, after a bank hold, until it is available to you. What's the solution to getting paid on time, or faster?

E D I

Yes, transmitting a document that contains all information, including the terms (the NET 10 or 30 part) in the document and the dates result in a clear-cut understanding of the milestones for this particular invoice.

So how does it work? Good question.

As with standard X12 EDI documents, there is an envelope that contains the:

ISA → GS → ST at the header

and the

SE → GE → IEA at the trailer

Since you all read and enjoyed book one of this series, that is all I plan to say about the envelope. You should understand it already.

But the invoice is actually a very simple document. More so than most other documents; however, yes, there are companies out there who attempt to make this the MOST complex document ever designed, requiring data from other documents that mean nothing in the invoice, it's just required because they want to feel powerful and make you jump through hoops to fulfill their requirements 100% to get paid. Remember, if your document does not contain everything they are looking for, they reject it. This, in and of itself, means you need to correct and resend the invoice which means it starts the 30-day timer to get paid all over again. I wonder if they actually used that unique data? Not going to talk about that either since we are here to discuss an electronic document that will get you paid fast and on time; not the inner workings of corporate Earth.

So, what's in an EDI Invoice, the 810 ANSI X12 EDI Document Set?

Let's take a fast look!

THE 810

This X12 Transaction Set establishes the data contents of the Invoice Transaction Set (810) for use in the context of an Electronic Data Interchange (EDI) environment. The transaction set is used to provide for the billing of goods and services provided.

The FUNCTIONAL GROUP is 'IN'

Remember in the Purchase order the first, and unique, segment is the BEG? In the invoice this unique segment is BIG.

BIG*20180601*374650001*20180520*X99W44**DI~

Let's review each of these elements in the BIG segment, and why they are needed.

A simple invoice contains 4 pieces of data, 2 dates and 2 ID numbers.

BIG01 = The date the invoice was issued
BIG02 = The invoice number assigned to this invoice
BIG03 = The date the PO was received
BIG04 = The PO number from the original PO
BIG07 = Designates a Debit Invoice to pay

If it were a CR, it would indicate a Credit Memo

From here you can add notes, and currency and communications contacts and yes, the BillTo and RemitTo address and information also.

We have already reviewed these fields in previous briefings, but as a recap, let's reinforce this information in the event you are new(er) to the world of EDI.

The N1-N2-N3-N4 segments tell us the WHO information, as in who bought it, who sold it, who does the purchaser remit payment to and a lot more that are rarely used. There are hundreds of qualifiers all over an EDI document including a ton of them in the N101 element, I will not list or talk about them all, that is not needed because under a standard document, there are very few that are used.

In book two, EDI – A Deeper Dive we discussed the purchase order but more so, and relevant to this briefing, we discussed the name segments. The N? segment.

So, how can you tell where to send the payment for the items that were ordered? You look at the N1 segment, and find the N101 when it is an RE. Simple, right. Let me elaborate.

The normal data you see for the place to Remit To, or RE is:

```
N1*RE*World Widgits*92*15668944~
N3*P.O. Box 951951~
N4*Austell*GA*30168-9123*USA~
```

So, in this instance, World Widgits sold and shipped the item, and would like for you to pay for what they sent, and you received.

Breaking this down so you can see what the parts are:

N101 = RE
N102 = World Widgits
N103 = 92
N104 = 15668944

But what exactly are these pieces? The N101 is the qualifier for the N102, just as the N103 is the qualifier for the N104. If the N101 is 'RE', or RemitTo then the N102 is the name of the company to send payment to. The N103 of 92 means the N104 is the Identification number or the seller number - as assigned by the buyer.

If it was a 1, then it would be their DUNS Number (Dun and Bradstreet) which identifies their company on the world marketplace. Every company has one and they are available and can be found on the internet easily.

It is easy to recognize that the N3 and the N4 contain the remainder of the RemitTo address like they are sending a check by mail, for example. N3 is the street address and the N401 is the City, the N402 is the state, the N403 is the zip code (yes, the zip code can be either a 5-digit number, or 9 or 10-digit number with or without the dash.

Most companies do not use the N404, which is the standard country code; USA, CAD, MEX etc.....

This N1-N3-N4 data set can loop many times, each giving a new piece of data. The N3 and N4 information can be a new address and it is designated by the N101 element. In an invoice, common N-Loops are:

When the....

> N101 is BY, it would be the Buying Party's address;
> N101 is SU, that is the Supplier's address;
> N101 is BT, it would be the Bill To address;
> N101 is.... well.... you get the idea. The list goes on.

There are more than 1,500 codes you can use in this element and each of them mean something unique.

One thing about these codes. If you use one, make certain your trading partner can read and understand it. If you are a Psychiatric Health Facility and use a 1W in the N101, that may be all well and good, but will your vendor understand that this is where you want it to be shipped to? Maybe, maybe not. That is the reason all of this is pre-defined in an implementation guide. You can go online and search for any 850 Implementation Guide and check one out.

One last thing about the addressing information, there is also an N2 segment that is not used all that often. It does nothing more than contain two elements, both text and all they are is additional name information.

So, if you saw the N1 and the N2

N1*RE*World Widgits*92*15668944~
N2*c/o Ramona O'Roury*AR Department~

This will let you know that the company is World Widgits and Ramona is assigned to accounting functions for this invoice. The N3 and N4 give you the physical address of where to mail the check.

So, you see, there can be a lot of information packed into a few lines like below. I bet you can understand exactly what you are reading now, right? Better than a few minutes ago, I'm sure of it!

```
N1*BT*World Widgits*~
N3*P.O. Box 951000~
N4*Austell*GA*30168-9123*USA~
N1*RE*World Widgits*92*15668944~
N2*c/o Bob Williams*AR Dept~
N3*P.O. Box 951951~
N4*Austell*GA*30168-9123*USA~
N1*BY*Widgits Makerz*92*5645~
N3*159 Central Street~
N4*Cleveland*OH*44110-5478*USA~
```

How did you do? GREAT!!!

Next and last in the HEADER is the ITD, which details the terms. Look below, the '05' means Discount is not Applicable and the 'ZZ' means mutually defined. So, the 30 has to mean Net Term in Days. That's it. Pay it 30 days from the invoice date, simple!

```
ITD*05*ZZ*30~
```

So, if the invoice date in the BIG01 is 20180601, then the date payment needs to be received is 20180701. What could be easier to understand.

Sadly, there are organizations that stockpile invoices to be paid and sort them by the final date due; therefore, if they send the check on that date there would be no penalty. Like playing with fire, eventually you get burned!

SO, that's the header. What's next, the detail of course.

The Detail

The detail segments are the IT1 and the PID. The IT1 is the data about the items and the PID is the description.

```
IT1*010*12*EA*9.99**VP*EDI001-001*IB*978-1973550709~
PID*F****EDI - Electronic Data Interchange - An introduction~
```

The IT101 is a line counter, preferably the same line number as indicated on the original 850 purchase order document.

The next three all relate. IT102 contains the number that were purchased, so in this instance a dozen, 12, were purchased. The IT103 tells us the unit of measure, so EACH (EA) and the IT104 has the unit price.

Therefore, a total of 12 each at a price of $9.99 for each one was purchased.

The IT105 is an optional segment. In this instance, it can be 'PE', which means Price Each. If it were 'PP', it would mean Price per Pound if ordering bulk beans or something. It is an optional element, so here it is not used.

The IT106 and IT107 go together, as do the IT108 and the IT109. They contain the identification numbers of the item purchased. In this instance we have two distinct codes. We have the 'VP' and the 'IB'.

The 'VP' is the Vendor Part Number. So, the seller puts their part number into the file. The 'IB' is the ISBN number, so we know the item purchased is a book.

There are a lot more qualifiers that can be used or added, but are they necessary? Only if you are your trading partner want them included.

The PID segment is the description. PID01, being an 'F' means it is FreeForm Text, and the text is in PID05; so the name of the book being purchased.

One note, in the actual name of the book in this instance, the real title of the book is "E*D*I: Electronic Data Interchange – An Introduction"

Why is it different than the title in the PID segment?

Think about it a for a minute, then read on............

====================================

Did you figure it out? Yep, you got it.

Putting an asterisk in the text of the PID segment means a new element, and the EDI when received should blow up. And the colon, that is normally used for the sub-element separator as defined in the ISA segment of the EDI document. You can use a colon in the data "IF" you put a '>' in the ISA as the Sub-Element Separator.

OK, that's all that's needed in the detail, and the trailer or summary segment is all that is left.

The Summary

The TDS segment is next.

That is the PAY THIS AMOUNT segment, and only the TDS01 is really needed. So, in this case, the 23976 actually means $239.76; if you multiply the IT102 by the IT104, what do you get?

The CTT segment has two entries. The CTT01 is the Line Item Total, or the count of the number of IT1 segemtns in the document, or the number of items ordered (not the total number, but unique line items).

The CTT02 is called a hash total, and it adds up the number of items that were shipped and need to be paid on this invoice. So, if there are 2-line items, and 12 in each line item ordered; a CTT*2*24 means two different items totaling 24 shipped eaches.

In Closing

OK, that's it.

You now understand a BASIC invoice.

There are a lot of things you can add to enhance, or even convolute, the document but that is between you and your trading partner to hash out.

I hope you enjoyed this briefing, and I hope you read all of the books in my EDI Education Series

APPENDIX "A"

```
ST*810*0001~
BIG*20180601*374650001*20180520*X99W44**DI~
N1*BT*World Widgits*~
N3*P.O. Box 951000~
N4*Austell*GA*30168-9123*USA~
N1*RE*World Widgits*92*15668944~
N2*c/o Bob Williams*AR Dept~
N3*P.O. Box 951951~
N4*Austell*GA*30168-9123*USA~
N1*BY*Widgits Makerz*92*5645~
N3*159 Central Street~
N4*Cleveland*OH*44110-5478*USA~
ITD*05*ZZ*30~
IT1*010*12*EA*9.99**VP*EDI001-001*IB*978-1973550709~
PID*F****EDI - Electronic Data Interchange - An introduction~
IT1*020*12*EA*9.99**VP*EDI002-002*IB*978-1983115042~
PID*F****EDI - A Deeper Dive - Dissecting the 850 Purchase Order~
SLN*00010**O~
TDS*23976~
CTT*2*24~
SE*12*0001~
```

Additional Works by

Christopher E. Cancilla

The Archives, a 7-Part Series of Novels

The ARCHIVES: Education

Book One in the Archives Series.

Benjamin Jensen is a temporal researcher, a good one. His career started out rough when he nearly destroyed all of history or lost the love of his life in a tragic accident which could have been prevented by him later in his career; but things have a way of working out. His favorite flight home is on the drop-ship from low Earth orbit, and he try's as hard as he can to get anyone to join him. His close friends run the Flight Dome on Lunar Base, where flapping and flying like a bird is commonplace and a fun pastime, but his real passion is for historical events.... or more precisely the events surrounding and leading up to the actual event in focus. Join Benjamin Jensen and his classmates as they discover what it means to be a Temporal Researcher. Find out the dangers and rewards this life could offer in an adventure with historical importance.

The ARCHIVES: Fixing Time

Book Two in the Archives Series.

Benjamin Jensen's best friend in all of time, Brad Jorgen, returns from a long-term research project with important news. Someone is traveling in time disrupting the time stream. Benjamin and Brad are tasked to repair and insure it does not happen again. Afterwards, the Archive Academy requests that the two of them teach a course in how to be inconspicuous when performing research, and how to improvise when things do not go as planned. The class is a hit, but there are a lot of bumps during the learning process. Including a covert trip to Pluto to reclaim a ship they left on the once and former planet several thousands of years earlier, one they will need to use to revive a civilization which has been dead and forgotten to the passage of time for several millennia.

Book Three in the Archives Series.
Several places on the Earth, the orbital facilities, the Lunar Colonies, and the far-reaching corners of the human populated universe, Christianity is beginning to grow, and spread. The world government is concerned it may over shadow their power, or their ability to lead the people into their vision of what the future needs to look like. Benjamin is tasked to determine the threat-level of this new group and he and his team of one is sent back to a place where the movement begins. Is this movement mind altering or simple brainwashing? Do Christians want to control everything? Is there a reason to fear Christians, or all religion in general? This is what he is tasked to learn, and fix, if necessary. On the way, he discovers a unique reality and brings that information back to his boss at Archive Island, in the form of a very interesting, honest and convincing report. Enveloped within this decision is his new wife, and his best friend in all of time. Come and be with him as he explores his heart and his mind. The scientist needs to understand the definition of faith, and faith can be elusive.

Book Four in the Archives Series.

Benjamin Jensen is selected to take over as the Director of the entire Archive Island complex, including all operations and locations. With that promotion comes both amazing responsibility in the guise of becoming one of the most powerful men in history, and a danger so terrifying it has never before surfaced. With his promotion means that each of his compatriots are promoted to fill in the void as he and Brad Jorgen are propelled into intrigue and mystery. The big questions on everyone's lips, will Benjamin measure up to match the job? Can Brad avert a disaster that could mean an end to the Jensen lineage? Why a reporter is permitted free run of the Archive Island complex is baffling to some, but allowed to happen by all? Come and take this journey with us to explore the dark areas of space and the human condition, and the soft spots in our Family.

Book Five in the Archives Series.

Benjamin Jensen is the Director of the Island Complex for nearly two decades now, and his best friend Brad Jorgen is his second-in-command. Their sons are students in the Academy and already well on their way to becoming influential and experienced members of the Archive Island Complex Temporal Research team. But, is there danger? Can they trust a non-TR with the secrets of temporal research? Will they need to correct time so history can flow as it is intended? Join the journey....join the excitement.

Book Six in the Archives Series.
Benjamin Jensen is still the Director of the
Island Complex. It has been a bit more than
30 years. With the unexpected death of
someone close, the Island is turned on its
ear. Recalling several people close, the
memorial service is brief, but the grieving is
deep.

This is the sixth and final book in the series
that traverses the TR lifetime of Benjamin
Jensen, his family, and his friends.

Book Seven in the Archives Series.

This closes out the Archive Series with flare. Not a continuation of the story, but rather stories between what happens in the six previous installments of the Archive Series.

Each character we have come to love and adore has a tribute in this book, each of them has a story that revolves around them that occurs between the stories you are familiar with. Read and learn about the favorite saga in the life of your favorite characters.

Discover something no one knew before.

Business books by Christopher E. Cancilla

E*D*I: A Simple Introduction

A briefing on what EDI is, and how it works

EDI can and is difficult for the uninitiated to read. It is a "digital" representation of a human readable document, like a purchase order for example. By reading this short introduction into the world of EDI you will understand how it is structured, why it is necessary, what a standard is and what the individual pieces of data mean and how they interrelate.

Welcome to EDI-101

E*D*I: A Deeper Dive

A briefing on the Purchase Order

EDI may be a mystery, but then again so is magic until you know how the illusion is done. Take the 850-document set, the purchase order. What is it, what are the moving parts and what do all those parts mean? Take a ride with me through the PO. Let's explore how the 850 is put together and learn in the process. Remember, EDI is FUN!!

E*D*I: Getting Paid

A briefing on the Invoice

Selling and buying is called commerce, and when using EDI, you are involved in Electronic Commerce. So, read about how to simplify your invoicing, cut costs by not having to create, print, address envelopes, and mail invoices to your customers.

Learn how an electronic invoice can get you paid faster.

E*D*I: Shipping and the Notice

A briefing on the Advanced Ship Notice

The ASN, or 856, is seriously one of the most misunderstood documents in EDI. People try to avoid them like the plague. Why? They don't understand them.

If you understood the ASN, the 856, you would be comfortable reading, and yes mapping, the 856 into your repertoire of documents.

Learn how easy it is to create an electronic ASN.

Other Novels by Christopher E. Cancilla

Bus Route 40-A

A novel
The life of a planetary bus driver can be mundane, repetitious, sedate, and of course unique, interesting, exciting and spontaneous. Driving your whale around the planet picking people up and dropping them off is a lot of fun, sure. But at the same time it is good to get a break in the monotonous time you call your day. So when Walt was asked to take a charter trip for a few days, he jumped all over it, and knowing he had a good friend to ride shotgun, he felt like it would be a good thing. Plus, you get double pay and less work time so he could be home more after the trip was over. No could ever imagine what was about to happen, Walt would either survive the incident, or he would die. Either way, he would be hailed a hero.

The Cancilla Collection

A collection: short stories, essays, & ideas.
Chris Cancilla enjoys…no, he LOVES to write. And to that end he has an opinion on just about everything. You can enjoy an eclectic sampling of a small collection of some of the pros he has penned throughout his life.

Cookbooks Available by Christopher E. Cancilla

Camp Menu Planning

An Outdoor Cookbook

⁇⁇
⁇⁇⁇⁇⁇⁇⁇⁇⁇⁇⁇⁇⁇⁇⁇⁇⁇⁇⁇⁇⁇⁇⁇⁇⁇⁇⁇⁇

Designed essentially for Boy Scouts to learn the art – if not the technique – of cooking. Contains a lot of recipes, but more importantly the recipes are more a method or style than a road map to a meal. Borrowing one recipe and using the technique of another and possibly ingredients of a third is what real cooking is all about, and this book instills that knowledge in whoever reads, and uses it to learn or learn something new. The additional information contained in the book are highly useful in the troop cooking experience. This book will give your Scouts the arrows in their culinary quiver to make friends and family happy. Gaining the knowledge and experience to impress his fellow patrol members with each meal in the woods and provide the Scout with the ammunition to cook an amazing meal.

Personal Menu Planning

A Backpackers Guide to eating

In the woods, on a trail, you need to adapt to your surroundings. For example, it is not practical on the Appalachian Trail to drag a cooler behind you. So, how can you make good food and save weight? It is quite easy

if you know a few secrets. Read and learn
and enjoy the tasty ideas.